IN CONNEMARA

In Connemara

JOHN M. SYNGE

THE MERCIER PRESS
DUBLIN and CORK

The Mercier Press Ltd
4 Bridge Street, Cork
25 Lower Abbey Street, Dublin 1

ISBN 0 85342 583 3

Printed by Litho Press Co., Midleton, Co. Cork.

CONTENTS

FROM GALWAY TO GORUMNA

Some of the worst portions of the Irish congested districts — of which so much that is
contradictory has been spoken and written —
lie along the further north coast of Galway Bay,
and about the whole seaboard from Spiddal to
Clifden. Some distance inland there is a line of
railway, and in the bay itself a steamer passes in
and out to the Aran Islands; but this particular
district can only be visited thoroughly by driving
or riding over some thirty or forty miles of
desolate roadway. If one takes this route from
Galway one has to go a little way only to reach
places and people that are fully typical of
Connemara. On each side of the road one sees
small square fields of oats, or potatoes, or
pasture, divided by loose stone walls that are
built up without mortar. Wherever there are a few
cottages near the road one sees bare-footed
women hurrying backwards and forwards, with
hampers of turf or grass slung over their backs,
and generally a few children running after them,
and if it is a market-day, as was the case on the
day of which I am going to write, one overtakes

long strings of country people driving home
from Galway in low carts drawn by an ass or
pony. As a rule one or two men sit in front of
the cart driving and smoking, with a couple of
women behind them stretched out at their ease
among sacks of flour or young pigs, and nearly
always talking continuously in Gaelic. These
men are all dressed in homespuns of the grey
natural wool, and the women in deep madder-
dyed petticoats and bodices, with brown shawls
over their heads. One's first feeling as one comes
back among these people and takes a place, so to
speak, in this noisy procession of fishermen,
farmers, and women, where nearly everyone is
interesting and attractive, is a dread of any
reform that would tend to lessen their individu-
ality rather than any very real hope of improving
their well-being. One feels then, perhaps a little
later, that it is part of the misfortune of Ireland
that nearly all the characteristics which give
colour and attractiveness to Irish life are bound
up with a social condition that is near to penury,
while in countries like Brittany the best external
features of the local life − the r'ch embroidered
dresses, for instance, or the carved furniture −
are connected with a decent and comfortable
social condition.

About twelve miles from Galway one reaches
Spiddal, a village which lies on the borderland
between the fairly prosperous districts near Galway and the barren country further to the west.
Like most places of its kind, it has a double row
of houses — some of them with two storeys —
several public-houses with a large police barrack
among them, and a little to one side a coast-
guard station, ending up at either side of the
village with a chapel and a church. It was evening when we drove into Spiddal, and a little after
sunset we walked on to a rather exposed quay,
where a few weather-beaten hookers were moored with many ropes. As we came down none of
the crews were to be seen, but threads of turf-
smoke rising from the open manhole of the fore-
castle showed that the men were probably on
board. While we were looking down on them
from the pier — the tide was far out — an old
grey-haired man, with the inflamed eyes that are
so common here from the continual itching of
the turf-smoke, peered up through the manhole
and watched us with vague curiosity. A few
moments later a young man came down from a
field of black earth, where he had been digging a
drain, and asked the old man, in Gaelic, to
throw him a spark for his pipe. The latter dis-

appeared for a moment, then came up again
with a smouldering end of a turf sod in his hand,
and threw it up on the pier, where the young
man caught it with a quick downward grab
without burning himself, blew it into a blaze, lit
his pipe with it, and went back to his work.
These people are so poor that many of them do
not spend any money on matches. The spark of
lighting turf is kept alive day and night on the
hearth, and when a man goes out fishing or to
work in the fields he usually carries a lighted sod
with him, and keeps it all day buried in ashes or
any dry rubbish, so that he can use it when he
needs it. On our way back to the village an old
woman begged from us, speaking in English, as
most of the people do to anyone who is not a
native. We gave her a few halfpence, and as she
was moving away with an ordinary 'God save
you!' I said a blessing to her in Irish to show her
I knew her own language if she chose to use it.
Immediately she turned back towards me and
began her thanks again, this time with extraordinary profusion. 'That the blessing of God
may be on you,' she said, 'on road and on ridge-
way, on sea and on land, on flood and on mountain, in all the kingdoms of the world' — and so
on, till I was too far off to hear what she was

saying.

In a district like Spiddal one sees curious gradations of type, especially on Sundays and holidays, when everyone is dressed as their fancy leads them and as well as they can manage. As I watched the people coming from Mass the morning after we arrived this was curiously noticeable. The police and coastgards came first in their smartest uniforms; then the shopkeepers, dressed like the people of Dublin, but a little more grotesquely; then the more well-to-do country folk, dressed only in the local clothes I have spoken of, but the best and newest kind, while the wearers themselves looked well-fed and healthy, and a few of them, especially the girls, magnificently built; then, last of all, one saw the destitute in still the same clothes, but this time patched and threadbare and ragged, the women mostly barefooted, and both sexes pinched with hunger and the fear of it. The class that one would be most interested to see increase is that of the typical well-to-do people, but except in a few districts it is not numerous, and it is always aspiring after the dress of the shop-people or tending to sink down again among the paupers.

Later in the day we drove on another long stage to the west. As before, the country we

passed through was not depressing, though stony
and barren as a quarry. At every cross-roads we
passed groups of young, healthy-looking boys
and men amusing themselves with hurley or
pitching, and further back on little heights, a
small field's breadth from the road, there were
many groups of girls sitting out by the hour,
near enough to the road to see everything that
was passing, yet far enough away to keep their
shyness undisturbed. Their red dresses looked
peculiarly beautiful among the fresh green of the
grass and opening bracken, with a strip of sea
behind them, and, far away, the grey cliffs of
Clare. A little further on, some ten miles from
Spiddal, inlets of the sea begin to run in towards
the mountains, and the road turns north to
avoid them across an expanse of desolate bog far
more dreary than the rocks of the coast. Here
one sees a few wretched sheep nibbling in places
among the turf, and occasionally a few ragged
people walking rapidly by the roadside. Before
we stopped for the night we had reached another
bay coast-line, and were among stones again.
Later in the evening we walked out round
another small quay, with the usual little band of
shabby hookers, and then along a road that rose
in some places a few hundred feet above the sea;

and as one looked down into the little fields that lay below it, they looked so small and rocky that the very thought of tillage in them seemed like the freak of an eccentric. Yet in this particular place tiny cottages, some of them without windows, swarmed by the roadside and in the 'boreens,' or laneways, at either side, many of them built on a single sweep of stone with the naked living rock for their floor. A number of people were to be seen everywhere about them, the men loitering by the roadside and the women hurrying among the fields, feeding an odd calf or lamb, or driving in a few ducks before the night. In one place a few boys were playing pitch with trousers buttons, and a little further on half-a-score of young men were making donkeys jump backwards and forwards over a low wall. As we came back we met two men, who came and talked to us, one of them, by his hat and dress, plainly a man who had been away from Connemara. In a little while he told us that he had been in Gloucester and Bristol working on public works, but had wearied of it and come back to his country.

'Bristol,' he said, 'is the greatest town, I think, in all England, but the work in it is hard.'

I asked him about the fishing in the neigh-

bourhood we were in. 'Ah,' he said, 'there's little
fishing in it at all, for we have no good boats.
There is no one asking for boats for this place,
for the shopkeepers would rather have the
people idle, so that they can get them for a
shilling a day to go out in their old hookers and
sell turf in Aran and on the coast of Clare.' Then
we talked of Aran, and he told me of people I
knew there who had died or got married since I
had been on the islands, and then they went on
their way.

BETWEEN THE BAYS OF CARRAROE

In rural Ireland very few parishes only are increasing in population, and those that are doing so are usually in districts of the greatest poverty. One of the most curious instances of this tendency is to be found in the parish of Carraroe, which is said to be, on the whole, the poorest parish in the country, although many worse cases of individual destitution can be found elsewhere. The most characteristic part of this district lies on a long promontory between Cashla Bay and Greatman's Bay. On both coastlines one sees a good many small quays, with, perhaps, two hookers moored to them, and on the roads one passes an occasional flat space covered with small green fields of oats — with whole families on their knees weeding among them — or patches of potatoes; but for the rest one sees little but an endless series of low stony hills, with veins of grass. Here and there, however, one comes in sight of a fresh-water lake, with an island or two, covered with seagulls, and many cottages round the shore; some of them standing almost on the brink of the water, others a little higher up, fitted in among the rocks, and one or two standing out on the top of a ridge against the blue of the sky or of the Twelve Bens of Connaught.

At the edge of one of these lakes, near a school of lace or knitting — one of those that have been established by the Congested Districts Board — we met a man driving a mare and foal that had scrambled out of their enclosure, although the mare had her two off-legs chained together. As soon as he had got them back into one of the fields and built up the wall with loose stones, he came over to a stone beside us and began to talk about horses and the dying out of the ponies of Connemara. 'You will hardly get any real Connemara ponies now at all,' he said; 'and the kind of horses they send down to us to improve the breed are no use, for the horses we breed from them will not thrive or get their health on the little patches where we have to put them. This last while most of the people in this parish are giving up horses altogether. Those that have them sell their foals when they are about six months old for four pounds, or five maybe; but the better part of the people are working with an ass only, that can carry a few things on a straddle over her back.'

'If you've no horses,' I said, 'how do you get to Galway if you want to go to a fair or to market?'

'We go by the sea,' he said, 'in one of the hookers you've likely seen at the little quays while walking down by the road. You can sail to Galway if the wind is fair in four hours or less maybe; and the people here are all used to the sea, for no one can live in this place but by cutting turf in the mountains and sailing out to sell it in Clare or Aran, for you see yourselves there's no good in the land, that has little in it but bare rocks and stones. Two years ago there came a wet summer, and the people were worse off then than they are now maybe, with their bad potatoes and all; for they couldn't cut or dry a load of turf to sell across the bay, and there was many a woman hadn't a dry sod itself to put under her pot, and she shivering with cold and hunger.'

A little later, when we had talked of one or two other things, I asked him if many of the people who were living round in the scattered cottages we could see were often in real want of food. 'There are a few, maybe, have enough at all times,' he said, 'but the most are in want one time or another, when the potatoes are bad or few, and their whole store is eaten; and there are some who are near starving all times, like a widow woman beyond who has seven children with hardly a shirt on their skins, and they with nothing to eat but the milk from one cow, and a handful of meal they will get from one neighbour or another.'

'You're getting an old man,' I said, 'and do you remember if the place was as bad as it is now when you were a young man growing up?'

'It wasn't as bad, or a half as bad,' he said, 'for there were fewer people in it and more land to each, and the land itself was better at the time, for now it is drying up or something, and not giving its fruits and increase as it did.'

I asked him if they used bought manures.

'We get a hundredweight for eight shillings now and again, but I think there's little good in it, for it's only a poor kind they send out to the like of us. Then there was another thing they had in the old times,' he continued, 'and that was the making of poteen (illicit whisky), for it was a great trade at that time, and you'd see the police down on their knees blowing the fire with their own breath to make a drink for themselves, and then going off with the butt of an old barrel, and that was one seizure, and an old bag with a handful of malt, and that was another seizure, and would satisfy the law; but now they must have the worm and the still and a prisoner, and there is little of it made in the country. At that time a man would get ten shillings for a gallon, and it was a good trade for poor people.'

As we were talking a woman passed driving two young pigs, and we began to speak of them.

'We buy the young pigs and rear them up,' he said, 'but this year they are scarce and dear. And indeed what good are they in bad years, for how can we go feeding a pig when we haven't enough, maybe, for ourselves? In good years, when you have potatoes and plenty, you can rear up to two or three pigs and make a good bit on them; but other times, maybe, a poor man will give a pound for a young pig that won't thrive after, and then his pound will be gone, and he'll have no money for his rent.'

The old man himself was cheerful and seemingly fairly well-to-do; but in the end he seemed to be getting dejected as he spoke of one difficulty after another, so I asked him, to change the subject, if there was much dancing in the country. 'No,' he said, 'this while back you'll never see a piper coming this way at all, though

in the old times it's many a piper would be
moving around through those houses for a whole
quarter together, playing his pipes and drinking
poteen and the people dancing round him; but
now there is no dancing or singing in this place
at all, and most of the young people is growing
up and going to America.'

I pointed to the lace-school near us, and asked
how the girls got on with the lace, and if they
earned much money. 'I've heard tell,' he said,
'that in the four schools round about this place
there is near six hundred pounds paid out in
wages every year, and that is a good sum; but
there isn't a young girl going to them that isn't
saving up, and saving up till she'll have enough
gathered to take her to America, and then away
she will go, and why wouldn't she?'

Often the worst moments in the lives of these
people are caused by the still frequent outbreaks
of typhus fever, and before we parted I asked
him if there was much fever in the particular
district where we were.

'Just here,' he said, 'there isn't much of it at
all, but there are places round about where
you'll sometimes hear of a score and more
stretched out waiting for their death; but I
suppose it is the will of God. Then there is a

sickness they call consumption that some will die of; but I suppose there is no place where people aren't getting their death one way or other, and the most in this place are enjoying good health, glory be to God! for it is a healthy place and there is a clean air blowing.'

Then, with a few of the usual blessings, he got up and left us, and we walked on through more of similar or still poorer country. It is remarkable that from Spiddal onward — that is, in the whole of the most poverty-stricken district in Ireland — no one begs, even in a roundabout way. It is the fashion, with many of the officials who are connected with relief works and such things, to compare the people of this district rather unfavourably with the people of the poor districts of Donegal; but in this respect at least Donegal is not the more admirable.

AMONG THE RELIEF WORKS

Beyond Carraroe, the last promontory on the north coast of Galway Bay, one reaches a group of islands which form the lower angle of Connemara. These islands are little more than a long peninsula broken through by a number of small straits, over which, some twelve years ago, causeways and swingbridges were constructed, so that one can now drive straight on through Annaghvaan, Lettermore, Gorumna, Lettermullan, and one or two smaller islands. When one approaches this district from the east a long detour is made to get round the inner point of Greatman's Bay, and then the road turns to the south-west till one reaches Annaghvaan, the first of the islands. This road is a remarkable one. Nearly every foot of it, as it now stands, has been built up in different years of famine by the people of the neighbourhood working on Government relief works, which are now once more in full swing; making improvements in some places, turning primitive tracts into roadways in others, and here and there building a new route to some desolate village.

We drove many miles, with Costello and Carraroe behind us, along a bog-road of curious formation built up on a turf embankment, with broad grassy sods at either side — perhaps to make a possible way for the barefooted people— then two spaces of rough broken stones where the wheel-ruts are usually worn, and in the centre a track of gritty earth for the horses. Then, at a turn of the road, we came in sight of a dozen or more men and women working hurriedly and doggedly improving a further portion of this road, with a ganger swaggering among them and directing their work. Some of the people were cutting out sods from grassy patches near the road, others were carrying down bags of earth in a slow, inert procession, a few were breaking stones, and three or four women were scraping out a sort of sandpit at a little distance. As we drove quickly by we could see that every man and woman was working with a sort of hang-dog dejection that would be enough to make any casual passer mistake them for a band of convicts. The wages given on these works are usually a shilling a day, and, as a rule, one person only, generally the head of the family, is taken from each house. Sometimes the best worker in a family is thus forced away from his ordinary work of farming, or fishing, or kelp-making for this wretched remuneration at a time when his private industry is most needed. If this system of relief has some things in its favour, it is far from satisfactory in other ways, and is not always economical. I have been told of a district not very far from here where there is a ganger, an overseer, an inspector, a paymaster, and an engineer superintending the work of two paupers only. This is possibly an exaggerated account of what is really taking place, yet it probably shows, not too inexactly, a state of things that is not rare in Ireland.

A mile or two further on we passed a similar band of workers, and then the road rose for a few feet and turned sharply on to a long cause-way, with a swing-bridge in the centre, that led to the island of Annaghvaan. Just as we reached the bridge our driver jumped down and took his mare by the head. A moment later she began to take fright at the hollow noise of her own hoofs on the boards of the bridge and the blue rush of the tide which she could see through them, but the man coaxed her forward, and got her over without much difficulty. For the next mile or two there was a continual series of small islands and causeways and bridges that the mare grew accustomed to, and trotted gaily over, till we reached Lettermore, and drove for some distance through the usual small hills of stone. Then we came to the largest causeway of all, between Lettermore and Gorumna, where the proportion of the opening of the bridge to the length of the embankment is so small that the tide runs through with extraordinary force. On the outer side the water was banked up nearly a yard high against the buttress of the bridge, and on the other side there was a rushing, eddying torrent that recalled some mountain salmon-stream in flood, except that here, instead of the brown river-water, one saw the white and blue foam of the sea.

The remainder of our road to the lower western end of Gorumna led through hilly districts that became more and more white with stone, though one saw here and there a few brown masses of bog or an oblong lake with many islands and rocks. In most places, if one looked round the hills a little distance from the road, one could see the yellow roofs and white gables of cottages scattered everywhere through this waste of rock; and on the ridge of every hill one could see the red dresses of women who

were gathering turf or looking for their sheep or
calves. Near the village where we stopped things
are somewhat better, and a few fields of grass
and potatoes were to be seen, and a certain
number of small cattle grazing among the rocks.
Here also one is close to the sea, and fishing and
kelp-making are again possible. In the village
there is a small private quay in connection with
a shop where everything is sold, and not long
after we arrived a hooker sailed in with a cargo
of supplies from Galway. A number of women
were standing about expecting her arrival, and
soon afterwards several of them set off for
different parts of the island with a bag of flour
slung over an ass. One of these, a young girl of
seventeen or eighteen, drove on with her load far
into Lettermullan, the next island, on a road
that we were walking also; and then sent the ass
back to Gorumna in charge of a small boy, and
took up the sack of flour, which weighed at least
sixteen stone, on her back, and carried it more
than a mile, through a narrow track, to her own
home. This practice of allowing young girls to
carry great weights frequently injures them
severely, and is the cause of much danger and
suffering in their after lives. They do not seem,
however, to know anything of the risks they

run, and their loads are borne gaily.

A little further on we came on another stretch of the relief works, where there were many elderly men and young girls working with the same curious aspect of shame and dejection. The work was just closing for the evening, and as we walked back to Gorumna an old man who had been working walked with us, and complained of his great poverty and the small wages he was given. 'A shilling a day,' he said, 'would hardly keep a man in tea and sugar and tobacco and a bit of bread to eat, and what good is it at all when there is a family of five or six maybe, and often more?' Just as we reached the swing-bridge that led back to Gorumna another hooker sailed carefully in through the narrow rocky channel, with a crowd of men and women sitting along the gunwale. They edged in close to a flat rock near the bridge, and made her fast for a moment while the women jumped on shore; some of them carrying bottles, others with little children, and all dressed out in new red petticoats and shawls. They looked as they crowded up on the road as fine a body of peasant women as one could see anywhere, and were all talking and laughing eagerly among themselves. The old man told me in Irish that they had been at a

pattern — a sort of semi-religious festival like
the well-known festivals of Brittany — that had
just been held some distance to the east on the
Galway coast. It was reassuring to see that some,
at least, of these island people are, in their own
way, prosperous and happy. When the women
were all landed the swing-bridge was pushed
open, and the hooker was poled through to the
bay on the north side of the islands. Then the
men moored her and came up to a little public-
house, where they spent the rest of the evening
talking and drinking and telling stories in Irish.

THE FERRYMAN OF DINISH ISLAND

When wandering among lonely islands in the west of Ireland, like those of the Gorumna group, one seldom fails to meet with some old sailor or pilot who has seen something of the world, and it is often from a man of this kind that one learns most about the island or hill that he has come back to, in middle age or towards the end of his life. An old seafaring man who ferries chance comers to and from Dinish Island is a good example of this class. The island is separated from Furnace — the last of the group that is linked together by causeways and bridges — by a deep channel between two chains of rock. As we went to this channel across a strip of sandhill a wild-looking old man appeared at the other side, and began making signs to us and pushing off a heavy boat from the shore. Before he was half-way across we could hear him calling out to us in a state of almost incoherent excitement, and directing us to a ledge of rock where he could take us off. A moment later we scrambled into his boat upon a mass of seaweed

that he had been collecting for kelp, and he
poled us across, talking at random about how he
had seen His Royal Highness the Duke of Edin-
burgh, and gone to America as interpreter for
the emigrants in a bad season twenty-one years
ago. As soon as we landed we walked across a
bay of sand to a tiny schoolhouse close to the
sea, and the old man turned back across the
channel with a travelling tea merchant and a
young girl who had come down to the shore. All
the time they were going across we could hear
him talking and vociferating at the top of his
voice, and then, after a moment's silence, he
came in sight again, on our side, running towards
us over the sand. After he had been a little while
with us, and got over the excitement caused by
the sudden arrival of two strangers — we could
judge how great it was by a line of children's
heads who were peeping over the rocks and
watching us with amazement — he began to talk
clearly and simply. After a few of the remarks
one hears from everyone about the loneliness of
the place, he spoke about the school behind us.

'Isn't it a poor thing,' he said, 'to see a school
lying closed up the like of that, and twenty or
thirty scholars, maybe, running wild along the
sea? I am very lonesome since that school was

closed, for there was a schoolmistress used to come for a long while from Lettermullan, and I used to ferry her over the water, and maybe ten little children along with her. And then there was a mistress living here for a long while, and I used to ferry the children only; but now she has found herself a better place, and this three months there's no school in it at all.'

One could see when he was quiet that he differed a good deal, both in face and in his way of speaking, from the people of the islands, and when he paused I asked him if he had spent all his life among them, excepting the one voyage to America.

'I have not,' he said; 'but I've been in many places, though I and my fathers have rented the sixth of this island for near two hundred years. My own father was a sailorman who came in here by chance and married a woman, and lived, a snug, decent man, with five cows or six, till he died at a hundred and three. And my mother's father, who had the place before him, died at a hundred and eight, and he wouldn't have died then, I'm thinking, only he fell down and broke his hip. They were strong, decent people at that time, and I was going to school — travelling out over the islands with my father ferrying me —

till I was twenty years of age; and then I went to
America and got to be a sailorman, and was in
New York, and Baltimore, and New Orleans, and
after that I was coasting till I knew every port and
town of this country and Scotland and Wales.'

One of us asked him if he had stayed at sea
till he came back to this island.

'I did not,' he said, 'for I went ashore once
in South Wales, and I'm telling you Wales
is a long country, for I travelled all a whole
summer's day from that place till I reached
Birkenhead at nine o'clock. And then I went
to Manchester and to Newcastle-on-Tyne, and
I worked there for two years. That's a rich
country, dear gentlemen, and when the payman
would come into the works on a Saturday you'd
see the bit of board he had over his shoulder
bending down with the weight of sovereigns he
had for the men. And isn't it a queer thing to be
sitting here now thinking on those times, and I
after being near twenty years back on this bit of
a rock that a dog wouldn't look at, where the
pigs die and the spuds die, and even the judges
and quality do come out and do lower our rents
when they see the wild Atlantic driving in across
the cursed stones.'

'And what is it brought you back,' I said, 'if

you were doing well beyond in the world?'

'My two brothers went to America,' he said, 'and I had to come back because I was the eldest son, and I got married then, and I after holding out till I was forty. I have a young family now growing up, for I was snug for a while; and then bad times came, and I lost my wife, and the potatoes went bad, and three cows I had were taken in the night with some disease of the brain, and they swam out and were drowned in the sea. I got back their bodies in the morning, and took them down to a gentleman beyond who understands the diseases of animals, but he gave me nothing for them at all. So there I am now with no pigs, and no cows, and a young family running round with no mother to mind them; and what can you do with children that know nothing at all, and will often put down as much in the pot one day as would do three days, and do be wasting the meal, though you can't say a word against them, for it's young and ignorant they are? If it wasn't for them I'd be off this evening, and I'd earn my living easy on the sea, for I'm only fifty-seven years of age, and I have good health; but how can I leave my young children? And I don't know what way I'm to go on living in this place that the Lord

created last, I'm thinking, in the end of time;
and it's often when I sit down and look around
on it I do begin cursing and damning, and asking
myself how poor people can go on executing
their religion at all.'

For a while he said nothing, and we could see
tears in his eyes; then I asked him how he was
living now from one day to another.

'They're letting me out advanced meal and
flour from the shop,' he said, 'and I'm to pay it
back when I burn a ton of kelp in the summer.
For two months I was working on the relief
works at a shilling a day, but what good is that
for a family? So I've stopped now to rake up
weed for a ton, or maybe two tons, of kelp.
When I left the works I got my boy put on in
my place, but the ganger put him back; and then
I got him on again, and the ganger put him back.
Then I bought a bottle of ink and a pen and a
bit of paper to write a letter and make my com-
plaint, but I never wrote it to this day, for what
good is it harming him more than another? Then
I've a daughter in America has only been there
nine months, and she's sent me three pounds
already. I have another daughter, living above
with her married sister, will be ready to go in
autumn, and another little one will go when

she's big enough. There is a man above has four daughters in America, and gets a pound a quarter from each one of them, and that is a great thing for a poor man. It's to America we'll all be going, and isn't it a fearful thing to think I'll be kept here another ten years, maybe, tending the children and striving to keep them alive, when I might be abroad in America living in decency and earning my bread?'

Afterwards he took us up to the highest point of the island, and showed us a fine view of the whole group and of the Atlantic beyond them, with a few fishing-boats in the distance, and many large boats nearer the rocks rowing heavily with loads of weed. When we got into the ferry again the channel had become too deep to pole, and the old man rowed with a couple of long sweeps from the bow.

'I go out alone in this boat,' he said, as he was rowing, 'across the bay to the northern land. There is no other man in the place that would do it, but I'm a licensed pilot these twenty years, and a seafaring man.'

Then as we finally left him he called after us:

'It has been a great consolation to me, dear gentlemen, to be talking with your like, for one sees few people in this place, and so may God

bless and reward you and see you safely to your
homes.'

THE KELP MAKERS

Some of those who have undertaken to reform the congested districts have shown an unfortunate tendency to give great attention to a few canonised industries, such as horse-breeding and fishing, or even bee-keeping, while they neglect local industries that have been practised with success for a great number of years. Thus, in the large volume issued a couple of years ago by the Department of Agriculture and Technical Instruction for Ireland, which claims to give a comprehensive account of the economic resources of the country, hardly a word has been said of the kelp industry, which is a matter of the greatest importance to the inhabitants of a very large district. The Congested Districts Board seems to have left it on one side also, and in the Galway neighbourhood, at least, no steps appear to have been taken to ensure the people a fair market for the kelp they produce, or to revise the present unsatisfactory system by which it is tested and paid for. In some places the whole buying trade falls into the hands of

one man, who can then control the prices at his
pleasure, while one hears on all sides of arbitrary
decisions by which good kelp is rejected, and
what the people consider an inferior article is
paid for at a high figure. When the buying is thus
carried on no appeal can be made from the
decision of one individual, and I have sometimes
seen a party of old men sitting nearly in tears on
a ton of rejected kelp that had cost them weeks
of hard work, while, for all one knew, it had very
possibly been refused on account of some grudge
or caprice of the buyer.

The village of Trawbaun, which lies on the
coast opposite the Aran Islands, is a good
instance of a kelp-making neighbourhood. We
reached it through a narrow road, now in the
hands of the relief workers, where we hurried
past the usual melancholy line of old men breaking stones and younger men carrying bags of
earth and sods. Soon afterwards the road fell
away quickly towards the sea, through a village
of many cottages huddled together, with bare
walls of stone that had never been whitewashed,
as often happens in places that are peculiarly
poor. Passing through these, we came out on
three or four acres of sandhill that brought us to
a line of rocks with a narrow sandy cove between

them just filling with the tide. All along the coast, a little above high-water mark, we could see a number of tall, reddish stacks of dried sea-weed, some of which had probably been standing for weeks, while others were in various unfinished stages, or had only just been begun. A number of men and women and boys were hard at work in every direction, gathering fresh weed and spreading it out to dry on the rocks. In some places the weed is mostly gathered from the foreshore; but in this neighbourhood, at least in the early summer, it is pulled up from rocks under the sea at low water, by men working from a boat or curagh with a long pole furnished with a short crossbar nailed to the top, which they entangle in the weeds. Just as we came down a curagh, lightly loaded by two boys, was coming in over a low bar into the cove I have spoken of, and both of them were slipping over the side every moment or two to push their canoe from behind. Several bare-legged girls, crooning merry songs in Gaelic, were passing backwards and forwards over the sand, carrying heavy loads of weed on their backs. Further out many other curaghs, more heavily laden, were coming slowly in, waiting for the tide; and some old men on the shore were calling out directions

to their crews in the high-pitched tone that is so
remarkable in this Connaught Irish. The whole
scene, with the fresh smell of the sea and the
blueness of the shallow waves, made a curious
contrast with the dismal spectacle of the relief
workers we had just passed, for here the people
seemed as light-hearted as a party of schoolboys.

Further on we came to a rocky headland
where some men were burning down their weed
into kelp, a process that in this place is given
nearly twelve hours. As we came up dense
volumes of rich, creamy-coloured smoke were
rising from a long pile of weed, in the centre of
which we could see here and there a molten
mass burning at an intense heat. Two men and a
number of boys were attending to the fire, lay-
ing on fresh weed wherever the covering grew
thin enough to receive it. A little to one side a
baby, rolled up in a man's coat, was asleep
beside a hamper, as on occasions like this the
house is usually shut up and the whole family
scatters for work of various kinds. The amount
of weed needed to make a ton of kelp varies,
I have been told, from three tons to five. The
men of a family working busily on a favourable
day can take a ton of the raw weed, and the kelp
is sold at from three pounds fifteen shillings or

a little less to five pounds a ton, so it is easy to
see the importance of this trade. When all the
weed intended for one furnace has been used the
whole is covered up and left three or four days
to cool; then it is broken up and taken off in
boats or curaghs to a buyer. He takes a handful,
tests it with certain chemicals, and fixes the
price accordingly; but the people themselves
have no means of knowing whether they are
getting fair play, and although many buyers may
be careful and conscientious, there is a very
general feeling of dissatisfaction among the
people with the way they are forced to carry on
the trade. When the kelp has been finally dis-
posed of it is shipped in schooners and sent
away — for the most part, I believe, to Scotland,
where it is used for the manufacture of iodine.

Complaints are often heard about the idleness
of the natives of Connemara; yet at the present
time one sees numbers of the people drying and
arranging their weed until nightfall, and the bays
where the weed is found are filled with boats at
four or five o'clock in the morning, when the
tide is favourable. The chances of a good kelp
season depend, to some extent, on suitable
weather for drying and burning the weed; yet
on the whole this trade is probably less precari-

ous than the fishing industry or any other source of income now open to the people of a large portion of these congested districts. In the present year the weather has been excellent, and there is every hope that a good quantity of kelp may be obtained. The matter is of peculiar importance this year, as for the last few months the shopkeepers have been practically keeping the people alive by giving out meal and flour on the security of the kelp harvest — one house alone, I am told, distributed fourteen tons during the last ten days — so that if the kelp should not turn out well, or the prices should be less than what is expected, whole districts will be placed in the greatest difficulty.

It is a remarkable feature of the domestic finance of this district that, although the people are so poor, they are used to dealing with fairly large sums of money. Thus four or five tons of kelp well sold may bring a family between twenty and thirty pounds, and their bills for flour (which is bought in bags of two hundred-weight at a good deal over a pound a bag) must also be considerable. It is the same with their pig-farming, fishing, and other industries, and probably this familiarity with considerable sums causes a part, at least, of the sense of shame that

is shown by those who are reduced to working
on the roadside for the miserable pittance of
a shilling a day.

THE BOAT BUILDERS

We left Gorumna in a hooker managed by two
men, and saiiled north to another district of the
Galway coast. Soon after we started the wind
fell, and we lay almost becalmed in a curious
bay so filled with islands that one could hardly
distinguish the channel that led to the open sea.
For some time we drifted slowly between Dinish
Island and Illaunearach, a stony mound inhabited by three families only. Then our pace
became so slow that the boatmen got out a
couple of long sweeps and began rowing heavily,
with sweat streaming from them. The air was
heavy with thunder, and on every side one saw
the same smoky blue sea and sky, with grey
islands and mountains beyond them, and in one
place a ridge of yellow rocks touched by a single
ray of sunlight. Two or three pookawns — lateen-
rigged boats, said to be of Spanish origin —
could be seen about a mile ahead of us sailing
easily across our bows, where some opening in
the islands made a draught from the east. In
half an hour our own sails filled, and the boat-

44

men stopped rowing and began to talk to us.
One of them gave us many particulars about the
prices of hookers and their nets, and the system
adopted by the local boat-builders who work for
the poorer fishermen of the neighbourhood.

'When a man wants a boat,' he said, 'he buys
the timber from a man in Galway and gets it
brought up here in a hooker. Then he gets a
carpenter to come to his house and build it in
some place convenient to the sea. The whole
time the carpenter will be working at it the
other man must support him, and give him
whisky every day. Then he must stand around
while he is working, holding boards and handing
nails, and if he doesn't do it smart enough you'll
hear the carpenter scolding him and making a
row. A carpenter like that will be six weeks or
two months, maybe, building a boat, and he will
get two pounds for his work when he is done.
The wood and everything you need for a fifteen-
foot boat will cost four pounds, or beyond it, so
a boat like that is a dear thing for a poor man.'

We asked him about the boats that had been
made by the local boatwrights for the Congested
Districts Board.

'There were some made in Lettermullan,' he
said, 'and beyond in an island west of where

you're going today there is an old man has been
building boats for thirty years, and he could tell
you all about them.'

Meanwhile we had been sailing quickly, and
were near the north shore of the bay. The tide
had gone so far out while we were becalmed that
it was not possible to get in alongside the pier,
so the men steered for a ledge of rock further
out, where it was possible to land. As we were
going in an anchor was dropped, and then when
we were close to the rocks the men checked the
boat by straining on the rope, and brought us in
to the shore with a great deal of nicety.

Not long afterwards we made our way to the
old carpenter the boatman had told us of, and
found him busy with two or three other men
caulking the bottom of a boat that was propped
up on one side. As we came towards them along
the low island shore the scene reminded one
curiously of some old picture of Noah building
the Ark. The old man himself was rather remarkable in appearance, with strongly formed features,
and an extraordinarily hairy chest showing
through the open neck of his shirt. He told us
that he had made several nobbies for the Board,
and showed us an arrangement that had been
supplied for steaming the heavy timber needed

for boats of this class.

'At the present time,' he said, 'I am making
our own boats again, and the fifteen-foot boats
the people do use here have light timber, and we
don't need to trouble steaming them at all. I get
eight pounds for a boat when I buy the timber
myself, and fit her all out ready for the sea. But
I am working for poor men, and it is often three
years before I will be paid the full price of a
boat I'm after making.'

From where we stood we could see another
island across a narrow sound, studded with the
new cottages that are built in this neighbourhood by the Congested Districts Board.

'That island, like another you're after passing,
has been bought by the Board,' said the old
man, who saw us looking at them; 'and it is a
great thing for the poor people to have their
holdings arranged for them in one strip instead
of the little scattered plots the people have in all
this neighbourhood, where a man will often have
to pass through the ground of maybe three men
to get to a plot of his own.'

This rearrangement of the holdings that is being
carried out in most places where estates have
been bought up by the Board, and resold to the
tenants, is a matter of great importance that is

fully appreciated by the people. Mere tenant
purchase in districts like this may do some good
for the moment by lowering rents and interesting the people in their land; yet in the end it is
likely to prove disastrous, as it tends to perpetu-
ate holdings that are not large enough to support
their owners and are too scattered to be worked
effectively. In the relatively few estates bought
by the Board — up to March, 1904, their area
amounted to two or three hundred thousand
acres out of the three and a half million that are
included in the congested districts — this is being
set right, yet some of the improvements made at
the same time are perhaps a less certain gain, and
give the neighbourhoods where they have been
made an uncomfortable look that is, I think, felt
by the people. For instance, there is no pressing
need to substitute iron roofs — in many ways
open to objection — for the thatch that has been
used for centuries, and is part of the constructive
tradition of the people. In many districts the
thatching is done in some idle season by the men
of a household themselves, with the help of their
friends, who are proud of their skill; and it is
looked on as a sort of festival where there is
great talk and discussion, the loss of which is
hardly made up for by the patch of ground

which was needed to grow the straw, and is now free for other uses. In the same way, the improvements in the houses built by the Board are perhaps a little too sudden. It is far better, wherever possible, to improve the ordinary prosperity of the people till they begin to improve their houses themselves on their own lines, than to do too much in the way of building houses that have no interest for the people and disfigure the country. I remember one evening, in another congested district — on the west coast of Kerry — listening to some peasants who discussed for hours the proportions of a new cottage that was to be built by one of them. They had never, of course, heard of proportion; but they had rules and opinions, in which they were deeply interested, as to how high a house should be if it was a certain length, with so many rafters, in order that it might look well. Traditions of this kind are destroyed for ever when too sweeping improvements are made in a district, and the loss is a great one. If any real improvement is to be made in many of these congested districts the rearrangement and sale of the holdings to the tenants, somewhat on the lines adopted by the Board, must be carried out on a large scale; but in doing so care should be

taken to disorganise   as little as possible the life
and methods of the people. A little attention to
the wells, and, where necessary, greater assistance
in putting up sheds for the cattle and pigs that
now live in the houses, would do a great deal to
get rid of the epidemics of typhus and typhoid,
and then the people should be left as free as
free as possible to arrange their houses and way
of life as it pleases them.

THE HOMES OF THE HARVESTMEN

The general appearance of the North Mayo country round Belmullet — another district of the greatest poverty — differs curiously from that of Connemara. In Mayo a waste of turf and bog takes the place of the waste of stones that is the chief feature of the coast of Galway. Consequently sods of turf are used for all sorts of work — building walls and ditches, and even the gables of cottages — instead of the loose pieces of granite or limestone that are ready to one's hand in the district we have left. Between every field one sees a thin bank of turf, worn away in some places by the weather, and covered in others with loose grass and royal flowering ferns. The rainfall of Belmullet is a heavy one, and in wet weather this absence of stone gives one an almost intolerable feeling of dampness and discomfort.

The last forty miles of our journey to Belmullet was made on the long car which leaves Ballina at four o'clock in the morning. It was raining heavily as we set out, and the whole

51

town was asleep; but during the first hour we met many harvestmen with scythe-handles and little bundles tied in red handkerchiefs, walking quickly into Ballina to embark for Liverpool or Glasgow. Then we passed Crossmolina, and were soon out on the bogs, where one drives for mile after mile, seeing an odd house only, scattered in a few places with long distances between them. We had been travelling all night from Connemara, and again and again we dosed off into a sort of dream, only to wake up with a start when the car gave a dangerous lurch, and see the same dreary waste with a few wet cattle straggling about the road, or the corner of a lake just seen beyond them through a break in the clouds. When we had driven about fifteen miles we changed horses at a village of three houses, where an old man without teeth brought out the new horses and harnessed them slowly, as if he was half in his sleep. Then we drove on again, stopping from time to time at some sort of post-office, where a woman or boy usually came out to take the bag of letters. At Bangor Erris four more passengers got up, and as the roads were heavy with the rain we settled into a slow jog-trot that made us almost despair of arriving at our destination. The people were now at work weeding potatoes in their few patches of tillage, and cutting turf in the bogs, and their draggled, colourless clothes — so unlike the homespuns of Connemara — added indescribably to the feeling of wretchedness one gets from the sight of these miserable cottages, many of them with an old hamper or the end of a barrel stuck through the roof for a chimney, and the desolation of the bogs.

Belmullet itself is curiously placed on an isthmus — recently pierced by a canal — that divides Broad Haven from Blacksod Bay. Beyond the isthmus there is a long peninsula some fourteen miles in length, running north and south, and separating these two bays from the Atlantic. As we were wandering through this headland in the late afternoon the rain began again, and we stopped to shelter under the gable of a cottage. After a moment or two a girl came out and brought us in out of the rain. At first we could hardly see anything with the darkness of the rain outside and the small window and door of the cottage, but after a moment or two we grew accustomed to it, and the light seemed adequate enough. The woman of the house was sitting opposite us at the corner of the fire, with two children near her, and just behind them a large

wooden bed with a sort of red-covering, and red
curtains above it. Then there was the door, and a
spinning-wheel, and at the end opposite the fire
a couple of stalls for cattle and a place for a pig
with an old brood sow in it, and one young one
a few weeks old. At the edge of the fireplace a
small door opened into an inner room, but in
many cottages of this kind there is one apart-
ment only. We talked, as usual, of the hardships
of the people, which are worst in places like this,
at some distance from the sea, where no help
can be got from fishing or making kelp.

'All this land about here,' said the woman,
who was sitting by the fire, 'is stripped bog' —
that is, bog from which the turf has been cut —
'and it is no use at all without all kinds of stuff
and manure mixed through it. If you went down
a little behind the house you'd see that there is
nothing but stones left at the bottom, and you'd
want great quantities of sand and seaweed and
dung to make it soft and kind enough to grow a
thing in it at all. The big farmers have all the
good land snapped up, and there is nothing left
but stones and bog for poor people like ourselves.'

The sow was snorting in the corner, and I
said, after a moment, that it was probably with

the pigs that they made the most of their money.

'In bad years,' she said, 'like the year we've had, when the potatoes are rotten and few, there is no use in our pigs, for we have nothing to give them. Last year we had a litter of pigs from that sow, and they were little good to us, for the people were afraid to buy at any price for fear they'd die upon their hands.'

One of us said something of the relief work we had seen in Connemara.

'We have the same thing here,' she said, 'and I have a young lad who is out working on them now, and he has a little horse beast along with him, so that he gets a week's pay for three days or four, and has a little moment over for our own work on the farm.'

I asked her if she had many head of cattle.

'I have not, indeed,' she said, 'nor any place to feed. There is some small people do put a couple of yearlings out on the grass you see below you running out to the sands; but where would I get money to buy one, or to pay the one pound eight, or near it, you do pay for every yearling you have upon the grass? A while since,' she went on, 'we weren't so bad as we are at this time, for we had a young lad who used to go to Scotland for the harvest, and be

sending us back a pound or two pounds maybe
in the month, and bringing five or six or beyond
it when he'd come home at the end of the
autumn; but he got a hurt and never overed it,
so we have no one at this time can go from us at
all.'

One of the girls had been carding wool for the
spinning-wheel, so I asked about the spinning
and weaving.

'Most women spin their wool in this place,'
she said, 'and the weaver weaves it afterwards
for threepence a yard if it is a single weaving,
and for sixpence a yard if it is double woven, as
we do have it for the men. The women in this
place have little time to be spinning, but the
women back on the mountains do be mixing
colours through their woool till you'd never ask
to take your eyes from it. They do be throwing
in a bit of stone colour, and a bit of red madder,
and a bit of crimson, and a bit of stone colour
again, and, believe me, it is nice stuffs they do
make that you'd never ask to take your eyes
from.'

The shower had now blown off, so we went
out again and made our way down to a cove of
the sea where a seal was diving at some distance
from the shore, putting up its head every few

moments to look at us with a curiously human expression. Afterwards we went on to a jetty north of the town, where the Sligo boat had just come in. One of the men told us that they were taking over a hundred harvestmen to Sligo the next morning, where they would take a boat for Glasgow, and that many more would be going during the week. This migratory labour has many unsatisfactory features; yet in the present state of the country it may tend to check the longing for America that comes over those that spend the whole year on one miserable farm.

THE SMALLER PEASANT PROPRIETORS

The car-drivers that take one round to isolated places in Ireland seem to be the cause of many of the misleading views that chance visitors take up about the country and the real temperament of the people. These men spend a great deal of their time driving a host of inspectors and officials connected with various Government Boards, who, although they often do excellent work, belong for the most part to classes that have a traditional misconception of the country people. It follows naturally enough that the carmen pick up the views of their patrons, and when they have done so they soon find apt instances from their own local knowledge that give a native popular air to opinions that are essentially foreign. That is not all. The car-driver is usually the only countryman with whom the official is kept in close personal contact; so that, while the stranger is bewildered, many distinguished authorities have been pleased and instructed by this version of their own convictions. It is fair to add that the carman is usually a small-town's man, so that he has a not unnatural grudge against the mountain squatter, for whom so much has apparently been done, while the towns are neglected, and also that the carman may be generally relied on when he is merely stating facts to anyone who is not a total stranger to the country.

We drove out recently with a man of this class, and as we left Belmullet he began to talk of an estate that has been sold to the tenants by the Congested Districts Board.

'Those people pay one or two pounds in the year,' he said, 'and for that they have a house, and a stripe of tilled land, and a stripe of rough land, and an outlet on the mountain for grazing cattle, and the rights of turbary, and yet they aren't satisfied; while I do pay five pounds for a little house with hardly enough land to grow two score of cabbages.'

He was an elderly man, and as we drove on through many gangs of relief workers he told us about the building of the Belmullet Workhouse in 1857, and I asked him what he remembered or had heard of the great famine ten years earlier.

'I have heard my father say,' he said, 'that he often seen the people dragging themselves along to the workhouse in Binghamstown, and some

of them falling down and dying on the edge of
the road. There were other places where he'd
seen four or five corpses piled up on each other
against a bit of a bank or the butt of a bridge, and
when I began driving I was in great dread in the
evenings when I'd be passing those places on the
roads.'

It was a dark, windy day, and we went on
through endless wastes of brown mountain and
bog, meeting no one but an occasional woman
driving an ass with meal or flour, or a few
people drying turf and building it up into ricks
on the roadside or near it. In the distance one
could see white roads — often relief roads —
twisting among the hills, with no one on them
but a man here and there riding in with the mails
from some forlorn village. In places we could see
the white walls and gables of one of these villages
against the face of a hill, and fairly frequently
we passed a few tumbled-down cottages with
plots of potatoes about them. After a while the
carman stopped at a door to get a drink for his
horse, and we went in for a moment or two to
shelter from the wind. It was the poorest cottage
we had seen. There was no chimney, and the
smoke rose by the wall to a hole in the roof at
the top of the gable. A boy of ten was sitting

near the fire minding three babies, and at the other end of the room there was a cow with two calves and a few sickly-looking hens. The air was so filled with turf-smoke that we went out again in a moment into the open air. As we were standing about we heard the carman asking the boy why he was not at school.

'I'm spreading turf this day,' he said, 'and my brother is at school. Tomorrow he'll stay at home, and it will be my turn to go.'

Then an old man came up and spoke of the harm the new potato crop is getting from the high wind, as indeed we had seen ourselves in several fields that we had passed, where whole lines of the tops were broken and withered.

'There was a storm like this three weeks ago,' he said, 'and I could hardly keep my old bonnet on me going round through the hills. This storm is as bad, or near it, and wherever there are loops and eddies in the wind you can see the tops all fluttered and destroyed, so that I'm thinking another windy day will leave us as badly off as we were last year.'

It seems that about here the damage of the sea-winds, where there is no shelter, does as much or more harm than the blight itself. Still the blight is always a danger, and for several

years past the people have been spraying their
crops, with sufficiently good results to make
them all anxious to try it. Even an old woman
who could not afford to get one of the machines
used for this purpose was seen out in her field a
season or two ago with a bucketful of the solu-
tion, spraying her potatoes with an old broom —
an instance which shows how eager the people
are to adopt any improved methods that can be
shown to be of real value. This took place in the
neighbourhood of Aghoos — the place we were
driving to — where an estate has been bought by
the Congested Districts Board and resold to the
tenants. The holdings are so small that the rents
are usually about three pounds a year, though in
some cases they are much less, and it is easily
seen that the people must remain for a while at
least as poor, or nearly as poor, as they have
been in the past. In barren places of this kind
the enlarging of the holdings is a matter of the
greatest difficulty, as good land is not to be had
in the neighbourhood; and it is hard to induce
even a few families to migrate to another place
where holdings could be provided for them,
while their absence would liberate part of the
land in a district that is overcrowded. At present
most of the holdings have, besides their tilled

land, a stripe of rough bog-land, which is to be gradually reclaimed; but even when this is done the holdings will remain poor and small, and if a bad season comes the people may be again in need of relief. Still no one can deny the good that is done by making the tenants masters of their own ground and consolidating their holdings, and when the old fear of improvements, caused by the landlord system, is thoroughly forgotten, something may be done.

A great deal has been said of the curse of the absentee landlord; but in reality the small landlord, who lived on his property, and knew how much money every tenant possessed, was a far greater evil. The judicial rent system was not a great deal better, as when the term came to an end the careless tenant had his rent lowered, while the man who had improved his holding remained as he was — a fact which, of course, meant much more than the absolute value of the money lost. For one reason or another, the reduction of rents has come to be, in the tenants' view, the all-important matter; so that this system kept down the level of comfort, as every tenant was anxious to appear as poor as possible for fear of giving the landlord an advantage. These matters are well known; but at

the present time the state of suspended land-
purchase is tending to reproduce the same fear
in a new form, and any tenants who have not
bought out are naturally afraid to increase the
price they may have to pay by improving their
land. In this district, however, there is no fear of
this kind, and a good many small grants have
been given by the Board for rebuilding cottages
and other improvements. A new cottage can be
built by the occupier himself for a sum of about
thirty pounds, of which the Board pays only a
small part, while the cottages built by the Board
on their own plan, with slated roofs on them,
cost double, or more than double, as much. We
went into one of the reslated cottages with con-
crete floors, and it was curious to see that, however awkward the building looked from the outside, in the kitchen itself the stain of the turf-
smoke and the old pot-ovens and stools made
the place seem natural and local. That at least
was reassuring.

ERRIS

In the poorest districts of Connemara the people
live, as I have already pointed out, by various
industries, such as fishing, turf-cutting, and kelp-
making, which are independent of their farms,
and are so precarious that many families are
only kept from pauperism by the money that is
sent home to them by daughters or sisters who
are now servant-girls in New York. Here in the
congested districts of Mayo the land is still
utterly insufficient — held at least in small plots,
as it is now — as a means of life, and the people
get the more considerable part of their funds
by their work on the English or Scotch harvest,
to which I have alluded before. A few days ago a
special steamer went from Achill Island to Glasgow with five hundred of these labourers, most
of them girls and young boys. From Glasgow
they spread through the country in small bands
and work together under a ganger, picking
potatoes or weeding turnips, and sleeping for the
most part in barns and outhouses. Their wages
vary from a shilling a day to perhaps double as

much in places where there is more demand for
their work. The men go more often to the north
of England, and usually work together, where it
is possible, on small contracts for piecework
arranged by one of themselves until the hay
harvest begins, when they work by the day. In
both cases they get fairly good wages, so that if
they are careful and stay for some months they
can bring back eight or nine pounds with them.

This morning people were passing through the
town square of Belmullet — where our windows
look out — towards the steamer, from two
o'clock, in small bands of boys and girls, many
of them carrying their boots under their arms
and walking in bare feet, a fashion to which they
are more used. Last night also, on our way back
from a village that is largely inhabited by harvest
people, we saw many similar bands hurrying in
towards the town, as the steamer was to sail
soon after dawn. This part of the coast is cut
into by a great number of shallow tidal estuaries
which are dry at low tide, while at full tide one
sees many small roads that seem to run down
aimlessly into the sea, till one notices, perhaps
half a mile away, a similar road running down on
the opposite headland. On our way, as the tide
was out, we passed one of these sandy fords

where there were a number of girls gathering cockles, and drove into Geesala, where we left our car and walked on to the villages of Doo-york, which lie on a sort of headland cut off on the south by another long estuary. It is in places like this, where there is no thoroughfare in any direction to bring strangers to the country, that one meets with the most individual local life. There are two villages of Dooyork, an upper and lower, and as soon as we got into the first every doorway was filled with women and children looking after us with astonishment. All the houses were quite untouched by improvements, and a few of them were broken-down hovels of the worst kind. On the road there were several women bringing in turf or seaweed on horses with large panniers slung over a staw straddle, on which usually a baby of two or three years old was riding with delight. At the end of the village we talked to a man who had been in America, and before that had often gone to England as a harvestman.

'Some of the men get a nice bit of money,' he said, 'but it is hard work. They begin at three in the morning, and they work on till ten at night. A man will sometimes get twelve shillings an acre for hoeing turnips, and a skilful man will do

an acre or the better part of it in one day; but
I'm telling you it is hard work, and before the
day is done a man will be hard set to know if it's
the soil or the turnips he's striking down on.'

I asked him where and how they lodged.

'Ah,' he said, 'don't ask me to speak to you of
that, for the lodging is poor, surely.'

We went on then to the next village, a still
more primitive and curious one. The houses
were built close together, with passages between
them, and low, square yards marked round with
stones. At one corner we came on a group of
dark brown asses with panniers, and women
standing among them in red dresses, with white
or coloured handkerchiefs over their heads; and
the whole scene had a strangely foreign, almost
Eastern, look, though in its own way it was
peculiarly characteristic of Ireland. Afterwards
we went back to Geesala, along the edge of the
sea. This district has, unexpectedly enough, a
strong branch of the Gaelic League, and small
Irish plays are acted frequently in the winter,
while there is also an Agricultural Co-operative
Bank, which has done excellent work. These
banks, on the Raiffeisen system, have been
promoted in Ireland for the last nine or ten
years by the Irish Agricultural Society, with aid

from the Congested Districts Board, and in a small way they have done much good, and shown — to those who wished to question it — the business intelligence of the smallest tenant-farmers. The interest made by these local associations tends to check emigration, but in this district the distress of last year has a bad effect. In the last few months a certain number of men have sold out the tenant-right of their holdings — usually to the local shopkeeper, to whom they are always in debt — and shipped themselves and their whole families to America with what remained of the money. This is probably the worst kind of emigration, and one fears the sufferings of these families, who are suddenly moved to such different surroundings, must be great.

This district of the Erris Union, which we have now been through, is the poorest in the whole of Ireland, and during the last few months six or seven hundred people have been engaged on the relief works. Still, putting aside exceptionally bad years, there is certainly a tendency towards improvement. The steamer from Sligo, which has only been running for a few years, has done much good by bringing in flour and meal **much** more cheaply than could be done former-

ly. Typhus is less frequent than it used to be,
probably because the houses and holdings are
improving gradually, and we have heard it said
that the work done in Aghoos by the fund raised
by the *Manchester Guardian* some years ago was
the beginning of this better state of things. The
relief system, as it is now carried on, is an utterly degrading one, and many things will have to
be done before the district is in anything like a
satisfactory state. Yet the impression one gets of
the whole life is not a gloomy one. Last night
was St John's Eve, and bonfires — a relic of
Druidical rites — were lighted all over the
country, the largest of all being placed in the
town square of Belmullet, where a crowd of
small boys shrieked and cheered and threw up
firebrands for hours together. Today, again,
there was a large market in the square, where a
number of country people, with their horses and
donkeys, stood about bargaining for young pigs,
heather brooms, homespun flannels, second-
hand clothing, blacking-brushes, tinkers' goods
and many other articles. Once when I looked out
the blacking-brush man and the card-trick man
were getting up a fight in the corner of the
square. A little later there was another stir, and I
saw a Chinaman wandering about, followed by a

wondering crowd. The sea in Erris, as in Connemara, and the continual arrival of islanders and
boatmen from various directions, tend to keep
up an interest and movement that is felt even far
away in the villages among the hills.

THE INNER LANDS OF MAYO

THE VILLAGE SHOP

There is a curious change in the appearance of
the country when one moves inland from the
coast districts of Mayo to the congested portion
of the inner edge of the county. In this place
there are no longer the Erris tracts of bog or the
tracts of stone of Connemara; but one sees
everywhere low hills and small farms of poor
land that is half turf-bog, already much cut
away, and half narrow plots of grass or tillage.
Here and there one meets with little villages,
built on the old system, with cottages closely
grouped together and filled with primitive
people, the women mostly in bare feet, with
white handkerchiefs over their heads. On the
whole, however, one soon feels that this neighbourhood is far less destitute than those we have
been in hitherto. Turning out of Swinford, soon
after our arrival, we were met almost at once by
a country funeral coming towards the town,
with a large crowd, mostly of women, walking
after it. The coffin was tied on one side of an

outside car, and two old women, probably the chief mourners, were sitting on the other side. In the crowd itself we could see a few men leading horses or bicycles, and several young women who seemed by their dress to be returned Americans. When the funeral was out of sight we walked on for a few miles, and then turned into one of the wayside public-houses, at the same time general shop and bar, which are a peculiar feature of most of the country parts of Ireland. An old one-eyed man, with a sky-blue handkerchief round his neck, was standing at the counter making up his bill with the publican, and disputing loudly over it. Here, as in most of the congested districts, the shops are run on a vague system of credit that is not satisfactory, though one does not see at once what other method could be found to take its place. After the sale of whatever the summer season has produced — pigs, cattle, kelp, etc. — the bills are paid off, more or less fully, and all the ready money of a family is thus run away with. Then about Christmas time a new bill is begun, which runs on till the following autumn — or later in the harvesting districts — and quite small shopkeepers often put out relatively large sums in this way. The people keep no pass-books, so they have no

check on the traders, and although direct fraud
is probably rare it is likely that the prices charged
are often exorbitant. What is worse, the shopkeeper in out-of-the-way places is usually the
only buyer to be had for a number of home
products, such as eggs, chickens, carragheen
moss, and sometimes even kelp; so that he can
control the prices both of what he buys and
what he sells, while as a creditor he has an
authority that makes bargaining impossible:
another of the many complicated causes that
keep the people near to pauperism! Meanwhile
the old man's bill was made out, and the publican came to serve us. While he did so the old
man spoke to us about the funeral, and I asked
him about the returned Americans we had seen
going after it.

'All the girls in this place,' he said, 'are going
out to America when they are about seventeen
years old. Then they work there for six years or
more, till they do grow weary of that fixed kind of
life, with the early rising and the working late,
and then they do come home with a little stock-
ing of fortune with them, and they do be temp-
ting the boys with their chains and their rings, till
they get a husband and settle down in this place.
Such a lot of them is coming now there is hardly

a marriage made in the place that the woman hasn't been in America.'

I asked a woman who had come in for a moment if she thought the girls kept their health in America.

'Many of them don't,' she said, 'working in factories with dirty air; and then you have likely seen that the girls in this place is big, stout people, and when they get over beyond they think they should be in the fashions, and they begin squeezing themselves in till you hear them gasping for breath, and that's no healthy way to be living.'

When we offered the old man a drink a moment later, he asked for twopenny ale.

'This is the only place in Ireland,' he said, 'where you'll see people drinking ale, for it is from this place that the greatest multitudes go harvesting to England — it's the only way they can live — and they bring the taste for ale back along with them. You'll see a power of them that come home at Michaelmas or Martinmas itself that will never do a hand's turn the rest of the year; but they will be sitting around in each other's houses playing cards through the night, and a barrel of ale set up among them.'

I asked him if he could tell about how many

went from Swinford and the country round in
each year.

'Well,' he said, 'you'd never reckon them, but
I've heard people to say that there are six thousand or near it. Trains full of them do be running
every week to the city of Dublin for the Liverpool boat, and I'm telling you it's many are hard
set to get a seat in them at all. Then if the
weather is too good beyond and the hay is near
saved of itself, there is some that get little to do;
but if the Lord God sends showers and rain
there is work and plenty, and a power of money
to be made.'

While he was talking some men who were
driving cattle from a fair came in and sat about
in the shop, drinking neat glasses of whisky.
They called for their drinks so rapidly that the
publican called in a little barefooted girl in a
green dress, who stood on a box beside a porter
barrel rinsing glasses while he served the men.
They all appeared to know the old man with one
eye, and they talked to him about some job he
had been doing on the relief works in this district.
Then they made him tell a story for us of a
morning when he had killed three wild ducks
'with one skelp of a little gun he had,' and the
man who was sitting on a barrel at my side told

me that the old man had been the best shot in
the place till he got too fond of porter, and had
had his gun and his licence taken from him
because he was shooting wild over the roads.
Afterwards they began to make fun of him
because his wife had run away from him and
gone over the water, and he began to lose his
temper. On our way back an old man who was
driving an ass with heavy panniers of turf told us
that all the turf of this district will be cut away
in the next twenty years, and the people will be
left without fuel. This is taking place in many
parts of Ireland, and unless the Department of
Agriculture, or the Congested Districts Board,
can take steps to provide plantations for these
districts there may be considerable suffering, as
it is not likely that the people even then will be
able to buy coal. Something has been done and
a great deal has been said on the subject of growing timber in Ireland, but so far there has been
little result. An attempt was made to establish
an extensive plantation near Carna, in Connemara, first by the Irish Government in 1890, and
then by the Congested Districts Board since
1902; but the work has been a complete failure.
Efforts have been made on a smaller scale to
encourage planting among the people, but I have

not seen much good come of them. Some turf tracts in Ireland are still of great extent, but they are not inexhaustible, and even if turf has to be brought from them, in a few years, to cottagers great distances away, the cost of it will be a serious and additional hardship for the people of many poor localities.

THE SMALL TOWN

Many of the smaller towns of the west and south of Ireland — the towns chiefly that are in or near the congested districts—have a peculiar character. If one goes into Swinford or Charlestown, for instance, one sees a large dirty street strewn in every direction with loose stones, paper, and straw, and edged on both sides by a long line of deserted-looking shops, with a few asses with panniers of turf standing about in front of them. These buildings are mostly two or three storeys high, with smooth slate roofs, and they show little trace of the older sort of construction that was common in Ireland, although there are often a few tiny and miserable cottages at the ends of the town that have been left standing from an older period. Nearly all towns of this class are merely trading centres kept up by the country people that live round them, and they usually stand where several main roads come together from large, out-of-the-way districts. In Swinford, which may be taken as a good example of these market towns, there are seven roads leading into the country, and it is likely that a fair was started here at first, and that the town as it is now grew up afterwards. Although there is at present a population of something over 1,300 people, and a considerable trade, the place is still too small to have much genuine life, and the streets look empty and miserable till a market-day arrives. Then, early in the morning, old men and women, with a few younger women of about thirty who have been in America, crowd into the town and range themselves with their asses and carts at both sides of the road, among the piles of good which the shopkeepers spread out before their doors.

The life and peculiarities of the neighbour-hood — the harvesting and the potato blight, for instance — are made curiously apparent by the selection of these articles. Over nearly every shop door we could see, as we wandered through the town, two scythe-blades fixed at right angles over the doorways, with the points and edges uppermost, and in the street below them there were numbers of hay-rakes standing in barrels, scythe-handles, scythe-blades bound in straw rope, reaping-hooks, scythe-stones, and other things of the kind. In a smith's forge at the end of the town we found a smith fixing blades and hand-grips to scythe-handles for a crowd of men who stood round him with the blades and handles, which they had bought elsewhere, ready in their hands. In front of many shops also one could see old farmers bargaining eagerly for second-hand spraying machines, or buying supplies of the blue sulphate of copper that was displayed in open sacks all down the street. In other places large packing-cases were set up, with small trunks on top of them, and pasted over with advertisements of the various Atlantic lines that are used by emigrants, and large pictures of the Oceanic and other vessels. Inside many of the shops and in the windows one could see an extraordinary collection of objects —saddles, fiddles, rosaries, rat-traps, the Shorter Catechism, castor-oil, rings, razors, rhyme-books, fashion plates, nit-killer, and fine-tooth combs. Other houses had the more usual articles of farm and household use, but nearly all of them, even drapers' establishments, with stays and ribbons in the windows, had a licensed bar at the end, where one could see a few old men or women drinking whisky or beer. In the streets themselves there was a pig-market going on at the upper end of the town near the courthouse, and in another place a sale of barrels and churns,

made apparently by a local cooper, and also of
many-sized wooden bowls, pig-troughs, and the
wooden bars and pegs that are used on donkeys'
saddles to carry the panniers. Further down
there were a number of new panniers set out,
with long bundles of willow boughs set up
beside them, and offered for sale by old women
and children. As the day went on six or seven
old-clothes brokers did a noisy trade from three
large booths set up in the street. A few of the
things sold were new, but most of them were
more or less worn out, and the sale was carried
on as a sort of auction, an old man holding up
each article in turn and asking first, perhaps, two
shillings for a greasy blouse, then cutting away
the price to sixpence or even fourpence-half-
penny. Near the booths a number of strolling
singers and acrobats were lounging about, and
starting off now and then to sing or do contor-
tions in some part of the town. A couple of
these men began to give a performance near a
booth where we were listening to the bargaining
and the fantastic talk of the brokers. First one
of them, in a yellow and green jersey, stood on
his hands and did a few feats; then he went
round with his hat and sold ballads, while the
other man sang a song to a banjo about a girl:

. . . whose name it was, I don't know,
And she passed her life in a barber's shop
Making wigs out of sawdust and snow.

Not far away another man set up a stall, with
tremendous shouting, to sell some little packets,
and we could hear him calling out, 'There's
envelopes, notepaper, a pair of boot-laces, and
corn-cure for one penny. Take notice, gentlemen.'

At the time the braying of the asses that were
standing about the town was incessant and
extraordinarily noisy, as sometimes four or five
of them took it up at the same time. Many of
these asses were of a long-legged, gawky type,
quite unusual in this country, and due, we were
told, to a Spanish ass sent here by the Congested
Districts Board to improve the breed. It is unfortunate that most attempts to improve the live
stock of Ireland have been made by some off-
hand introduction of a foreign type which often
turns out little suited to the new conditions it is
brought to, instead of by the slower and less
exciting method of improving the different
types by selection from the local breeds. We
have heard a great deal in passing through
Connemara of the harm that has been done by
injudicious 'improving' of the ponies and horses,
and while it is probable that some of the object-

ions made to the new types may be due to local
prejudice, it should not be forgotten that the
small farmer is not a fool, and that he knows
perfectly well when he has an animal that is
suited to his needs.

Towards evening, when the market was beginning to break up, an outside car drove through
the town, laden on one side with an immense
American trunk belonging to a woman who had
just come home after the usual period of six
years that she had spent making her fortune. A
man at a shop door who saw it passing began to
talk about his own time in New York, and told
us how often he had had to go down to Coney
Island at night to 'recoup' himself after the heat
of the day. It is not too much to say that one
can hardly spend an hour in one of these Mayo
crowds without being reminded in some way of
the drain of people that has been and is still
running from Ireland. It is, however, satisfactory
to note that in this neighbourhood and west of
it, on the Dillon estate, which has been bought
out and sold to the tenants by the Congested
Districts Board, there is a current of returning
people that may do much good. A day or two
ago we happened to ask for tea in a cottage

which was occupied by a woman in a new American blouse, who had unmistakably come home recently from the States. Her cottage was perfectly clean and yet had lost none of the peculiar local character of these cottages. Almost the only difference that one could point to was a large photograph of the head of the Sistine Madonna, hanging over the fire in the little room where we sat, instead of the hideous German oleographs on religious subjects that are brought round by pedlars, and bought by most of the simpler Irish women for the sake of the subjects they represent

POSSIBLE REMEDIES

It is not easy to improve the state of the people in the congested districts by any particular remedy or set of remedies. As we have seen, these people are dependent for their livelihood on various industries, such as fishing, kelp-making, turf-cutting, or harvesting in England; and yet the failure of a few small plots of potatoes brings them literally to a state of famine. Near Belmullet, during a day of storm, we saw the crop for next year in danger of utter ruin, and if the weather had not changed, by good luck, before much harm was done, the whole demoralising and wretched business of the relief works would have had to be taken up again in a few months. It is obvious that the earnings of the people should be large enough to make them more or less independent of one particular crop, and yet, in reality, it is not easy to bring about such a state of things; for the moment a man earns a few extra pounds in a year he finds many good and bad ways of spending them, so that when a quarter of his income is cut away unexpectedly once in seven or eight years he is as badly off as before. To make the matter worse, the pig trade — which is often relied on to bring in the rent-money — is, as I have shown, dependent on the potatoes, so that a bad potato season means a dearth of food, as well as a business difficulty which may have many consequences. It is possible that by giving more attention to the supply of new seed potatoes and good manure — something in this direction is being done by the co-operative societies — the failure of the crop may be made less frequent. Yet there is little prospect of getting rid of the danger altogether, and as long as it continues the people will have many hardships.

The most one can do for the moment is to improve their condition and solvency in other ways, and for this purpose extended purchase on the lines adopted by the Congested Districts Board seems absolutely necessary. This will need more funds than the Board has now at its disposal, and probably some quicker mode of work. Perhaps in places where relief has to be given some force may have to be brought to bear on landlords who refuse to sell at fair terms. No amount of purchase in the poorer places will make the people prosperous — even if the hold-

ings are considerably enlarged — yet there is no
sort of doubt that in all the estates which the
Board has arranged and sold to the tenants there
has been a steady tendency towards improvement. A good deal may be done also by improved communications, either by railroad or by
sea, to make life easier for the people. For
instance, before the steamer was put on a few
years ago between Sligo and Belmullet, the cost
of bringing a ton of meal or flour by road from
Ballina to Belmullet was one pound, and one can
easily estimate the consequent dearness of food.
That is perhaps an extreme case, yet there are
still a good many places where things are almost
as bad, and in these places the people suffer
doubly, as they are usually in the hands of one
or two small shopkeepers, who can dictate the
price of eggs and other small articles which they
bring in to sell. At present a steamer running
between Westport and Belmullet, in addition to
the Sligo boat, is badly needed, and would
probably do a great deal of good more cheaply
than the same service could be done by a line of
railway. If the communications to the poorest
districts could be once made fairly satisfactory
it would be much easier for the Congested
Districts Board, or some similar body, to en-

courage the local industries of the people and to enable them to get the full market value for what they produce.

The cottage industries that have been introduced or encouraged by the Board — lacemaking, knitting, and the like — have done something; yet at best they are a small affair. In a few places the fishing industry has been most successfully developed, but in others it has practically failed, and led to a good deal of disappointment and wasted energy. In all these works it needs care and tact to induce the people to undertake new methods of work; but the talk sometimes heard of their sloth and ignorance has not much foundation. The people have traditional views and instincts about agriculture and live stock, and they have a perfectly natural slowness to adopt the advice of an official expert who knows nothing of the peculiar conditions of their native place. The advice given is often excellent, but there have been a sufficient number of failures in the work done by the Congested Districts Board, such as the attempt at forestry in Carna and the bad results got on certain of their example plots laid out to demonstrate the best methods of farming, to make the conservatism of the people a sign of, perhaps, valuable prudence. The Board and the Department of Agriculture and Technical Education have done much excellent work, and it is not to be expected that improvements of this kind, which must be largely experimental, can be carried on without failures; yet one does not always pardon a sort of contempt for the local views of the people which seems rooted in nearly all the official workers one meets with through the country.

One of the chief problems that one has to deal with in Ireland is, of course, the emigration that I have mentioned so often. It is probably the most complicated of all Irish affairs, and in dealing with it it is important to remember that the whole moral and economic condition of Ireland has been brought into a diseased state by prolonged misgovernment and many misfortunes, so that at the present time normal remedies produce abnormal results. For instance, if it is observed in some neighbourhood that the girls are going to America because they have no work at home, and a lace school is started to help them, it too often happens that the girls merely use it as a means of earning money enough to pay for their passage and outfit, and the evil is apparently increased. Further, it should not be forgotten that emigrants are going out at the present time for quite opposite reasons. In the poorest districts of all they go reluctantly, because they are unable to keep themselves at home; but in places where there has been much improvement the younger and brighter men and girls get ambitions which they cannot satisfy in this country, and so they go also. Again, where there is no local life or amusements they go because they are dull, and when amusements and races are introduced they get the taste for amusements, and go because they cannot get enough of them. They go as much from districts where the political life has been allowed to stagnate as from districts where there has been an excess of agitation that has ended only in disappointment. For the present the Gaelic League is probably doing more than any other movement to check this terrible evil, and yet one fears that when the people realise in five, or perhaps in ten, years that this hope of restoring a lost language is a vain one the last result will be a new kind of hopelessness and many crowded ships leaving Queenstown and Galway. Happily in some places there is a counter-current of people returning from America. Yet they are not very numerous, and one feels that the only real remedy for emigration is the restoration of some national life to the people. It is this conviction that makes most Irish politicians scorn all merely economic or agricultural reforms, for if Home Rule would not of itself make a national life it would do more to make such a life possible than half a million creameries. With renewed life in the country many changes of the methods of government, and the holding of property, would inevitably take place, which would all tend to make life less difficult even in bad years and in the worst districts of Mayo and Connemara.

MORE MERCIER BESTSELLERS

IN WEST KERRY
John M. Synge

The most exciting way to learn about West Kerry is to see it through the eyes of one of Ireland's greatest dramatists, J.M. Synge, and to let it weave its magic spell over us. He shows us the splendour of Kerry as we visit Dingle, Smerick Harbour, Sybil Ferriter's Castle, the Great Blasket, Tralee and we spend some time at the greatest event in Kerry — Puck Fair.

Synge invites us into the huts and cottages of the essentially Irish characters who had a dignity and settled peace that he not only noted but envied. According to Daniel Corkery Synge preferred the happy-go-lucky folks who were not authorities on anything and their rambling stories that had not a word of truth in them to the pronouncement of the wise. Their companion

to the pronouncements of the wise. Their companionship brings an unwonted delight and we relish the warmth of their hearts, their bright eyes, their reckless and astounding talk as they lead us far away from the stifling streets of the cities and towns. We joyfully go with them over the hillsides, into the mountainy glens and across the bogs.

It is a little star-dust caught; a segment of the rainbow which I have clutched.

THE WIND THAT ROUND THE FASTNET SWEEPS
John M. Feehan

There are moments in the life of every human being when he becomes haunted with the longing to leave behind the turmoil and tension of daily living, to get away from it all and to escape to a clime where true peace can be found. There are many practical reasons why most of us cannot do this so the next best thing is to read the story of one who tried.

John M. Feehan sailed, all by himself, in a small boat around the coast of West Cork in a search for this Land of the Heart's Desire, this Isle of the Blest.

The result is a book which is not only a penetrating spiritual odyssey, but also a magnificent account of the wild rugged coastline, the peaceful harbours, and the strange unique characters he met in this unspoiled corner of Ireland. He writes with great charm, skill, sympathy and a mischievous roguish humour often at his own expense. His sharp eye misses nothing. He sees the mystery, the beauty and the sense of wonder in ordinary things, and brings each situation to life so that the reader feels almost physically present during every moment of the cruise. '...brilliant... the Irish Story of San Michele.' — John.B. Keane.

THE MAGIC OF THE KERRY COAST
J.M. Feehan

This is a sequel to the best selling *The Wind That Round the Fastnet Sweeps*. In it John M. Feehan continues his odyssey from Crookhaven

up the coast of Kerry to the Skellig Rocks and the Blasket Islands. It follows the same pattern — a little sailing, a little thinking, a little laughing, a little drinking and once again we meet a marvellous collection of those strange and unusual characters who always seem to run across the author's path and which he describes with such understanding and humanity.
(June 1979).

RAMBLES IN THE WEST OF IRELAND
William Bulfin
William Bulfin takes us on a fascinating journey through the west of Ireland and we see haymaking, turf-cutting and enjoy a chat with the old people and listen to their stories. The reader will feel the pleasure of standing beside the graves of heroes and the ground made sacred by their heroism and will delight in visiting the banks of the Shannon. While reading this fascinating book it will be hard to remain in the present time as our thoughts will be far away while travelling the winding roads.

LETTERS FROM THE GREAT BLASKET
Eibhlis Ni Shulleabhain
A fascinating story of a strange and different way of life emerges in these letters which deal with the Great Blasket Island, its people and its

ways. They also include what must be an
almost unique specimen of 'The Islandman's'
writing in English.

THE MAN FROM CAPE CLEAR
Conchur O Siochain
Translated by Riobard P. Breatnach
Conchur O Siochain lived all his days on Cape
Clear, the southern outpost of an old and deep-
rooted civilisation. He lived as a farmer and as a
fisherman and his story portrays the life of the
island (Fastnet Rock's nearest neighbour). He
was a gifted man in many ways and developed
skills as a storyteller, a folklorist and a crafts-
man. The book is a collection of memories and
musings, topography and tales, descriptions of
old ways and crafts, and contains a fund of
seafaring yarns and lore.
The Man from Cape Clear has been acclaimed
as a greater book than *The Islandman*.

SUPERSTITIONS OF THE IRISH
COUNTRY PEOPLE
Padraic O'Farrell
A Collection of Ireland's best known superstitions:
Do you know why it is considered unlucky to meet a
barefooted man, to start out on a journey on the tenth
of November, to get married on a Saturday?
Irish country people believe that angels are always
present among them and that all good things — crops,
rain and so forth come from them. Bad spirits bring
sickness to humans and animals and pestilence to crops.
They do not speak of fairies on Wednesdays or Fridays
for on those days they could be present while still
being invisible.